WILDLIFE VIEWING AREAS

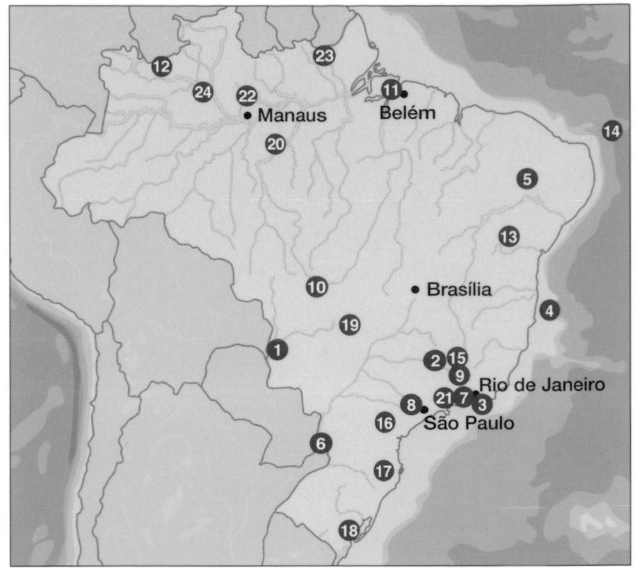

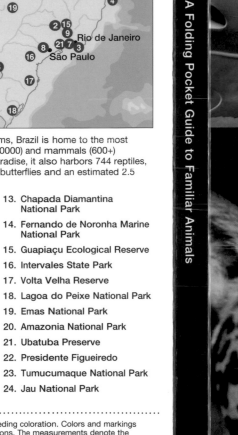

One of the world's richest ecosystems, Brazil is home to the most species of plants (55,000), fishes (3,0000) and mammals (600+) anywhere on earth. A naturalist's paradise, it also harbors 744 reptiles, 517 amphibians, 1,622 birds, 3,150 butterflies and an estimated 2.5 million species of insects.

1. Pantanal Biosphere Reserve
2. Serra da Canastra National Park
3. Tijuca National Park
4. Abrolhos Marine National Park
5. Caatinga Biosphere Reserve
6. Iguazu Falls
7. National Museum of Brazil
8. Museum of Zoology of the University of São Paulo
9. Itatiaia National Park
10. Chapada dos Guimaraes National Park
11. Museu Paraense Emílio Goeldi
12. Pico da Neblina National Park
13. Chapada Diamantina National Park
14. Fernando de Noronha Marine National Park
15. Guapiaçu Ecological Reserve
16. Intervales State Park
17. Volta Velha Reserve
18. Lagoa do Peixe National Park
19. Emas National Park
20. Amazonia National Park
21. Ubatuba Preserve
22. Presidente Figueiredo
23. Tumucumaque National Park
24. Jau National Park

Most illustrations show the adult male in breeding coloration. Colors and markings may be duller or absent during different seasons. The measurements denote the length of most animals from nose/bill to tail tip. Butterfly measurements denote wingspan. Illustrations are not to scale.

Waterford Press produces reference guides that introduce novices to nature, science, travel and languages. Product information and hundreds of educational games are featured on the website: **www.waterfordpress.com**

Scan for more info

Text and illustrations © 2016 by Waterford Press Inc. All rights reserved. Cover images © Shutterstock.

To order, call 800-434-2555.
For permissions, or to share comments, e-maileditor@waterfordpress.com.
For information on custom-published products, call 800-434-2555 or e-mail info@waterfordpress.com. 507203

ISBN 13 978-1-58355-990-1 $7.95 U.S.
UPC
10 9 8 7 6 5 4 3 2 1 Made in the USA

BRAZIL WILDLIFE – A Folding Pocket Guide to Familiar Animals

Kavanagh/Leung

A POCKET NATURALIST® GUIDE

BRAZIL WILDLIFE

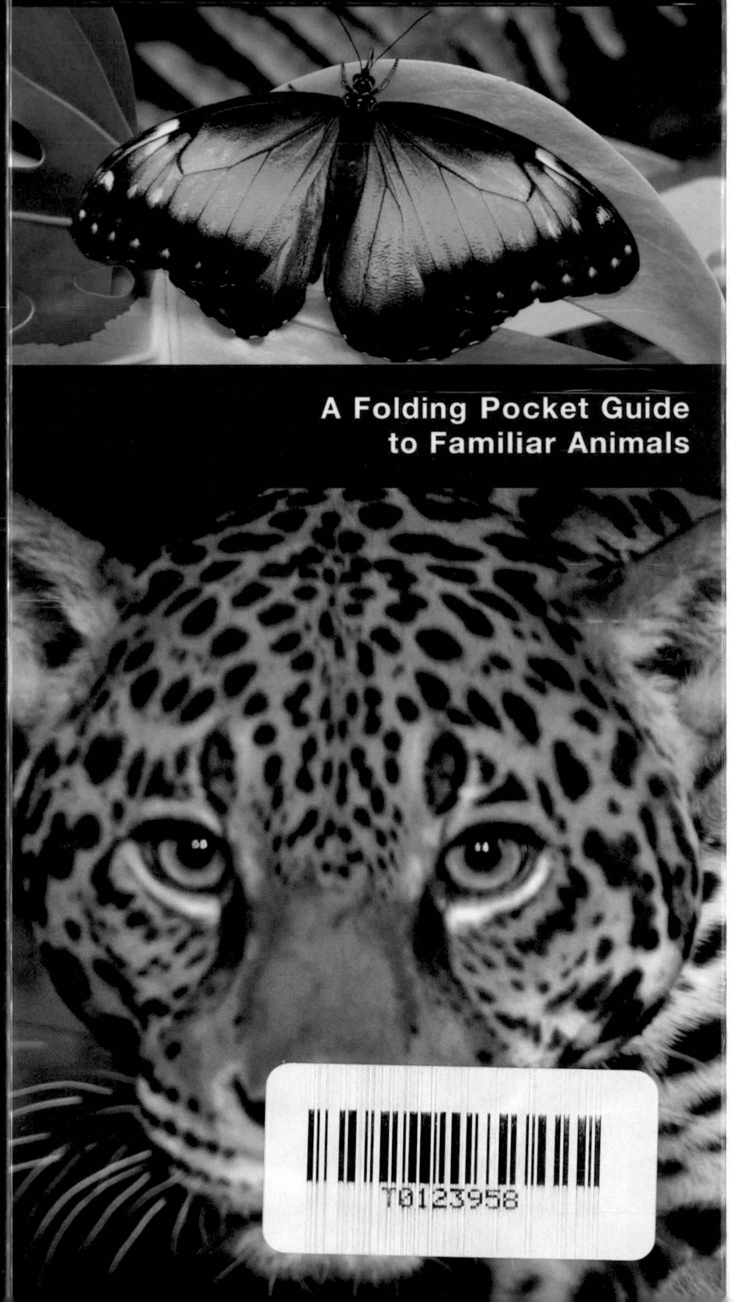

A Folding Pocket Guide to Familiar Animals

T0123958

BUTTERFLIES

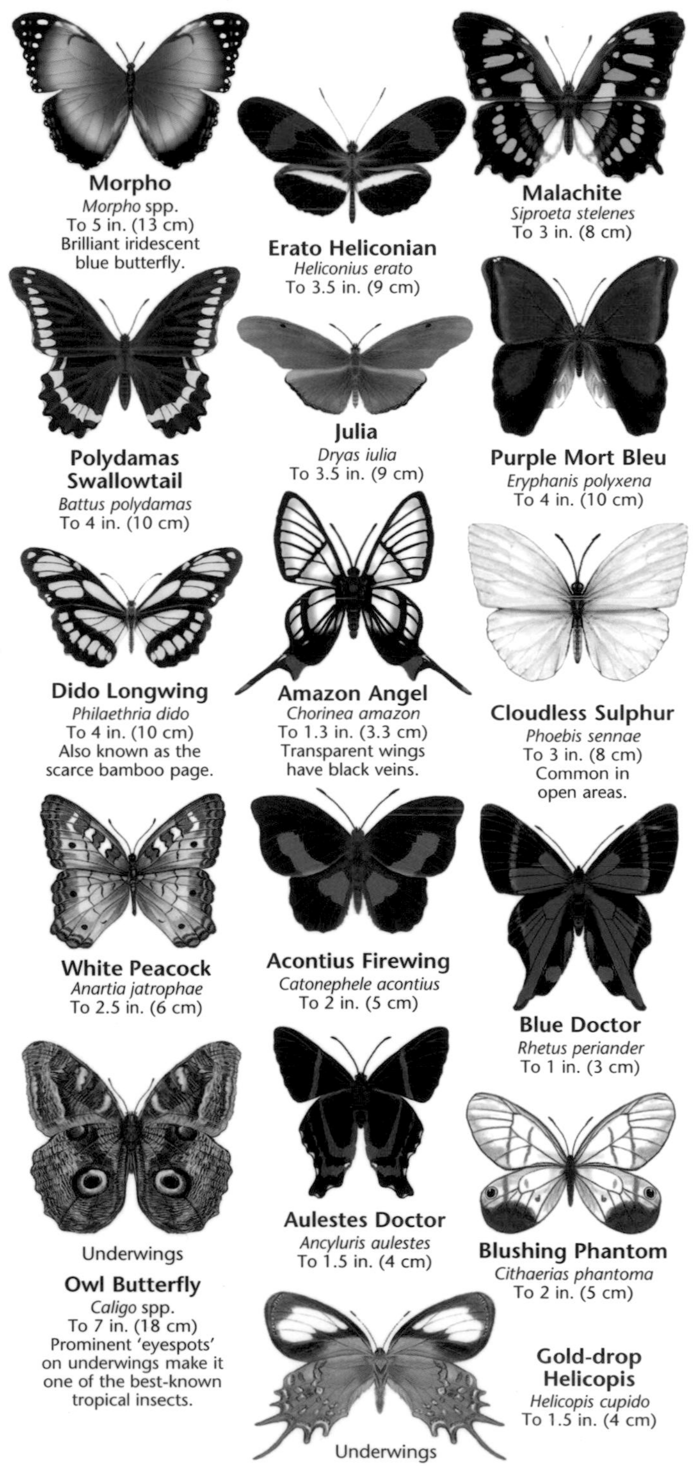

Morpho
Morpho spp.
To 5 in. (13 cm)
Brilliant iridescent blue butterfly.

Erato Heliconian
Heliconius erato
To 3.5 in. (9 cm)

Malachite
Siproeta stelenes
To 3 in. (8 cm)

Polydamas Swallowtail
Battus polydamas
To 4 in. (10 cm)

Julia
Dryas iulia
To 3.5 in. (9 cm)

Purple Mort Bleu
Eryphanis polyxena
To 4 in. (10 cm)

Dido Longwing
Philaethria dido
To 4 in. (10 cm)
Also known as the scarce bamboo page.

Amazon Angel
Chorinea amazon
To 1.3 in. (3.3 cm)
Transparent wings have black veins.

Cloudless Sulphur
Phoebis sennae
To 3 in. (8 cm)
Common in open areas.

White Peacock
Anartia jatrophae
To 2.5 in. (6 cm)

Acontius Firewing
Catonephele acontius
To 2 in. (5 cm)

Blue Doctor
Rhetus periander
To 1 in. (3 cm)

Underwings

Owl Butterfly
Caligo spp.
To 7 in. (18 cm)
Prominent 'eyespots' on underwings make it one of the best-known tropical insects.

Aulestes Doctor
Ancyluris aulestes
To 1.5 in. (4 cm)

Blushing Phantom
Cithaerias phantoma
To 2 in. (5 cm)

Gold-drop Helicopis
Helicopis cupido
To 1.5 in. (4 cm)

Underwings

INSECTS

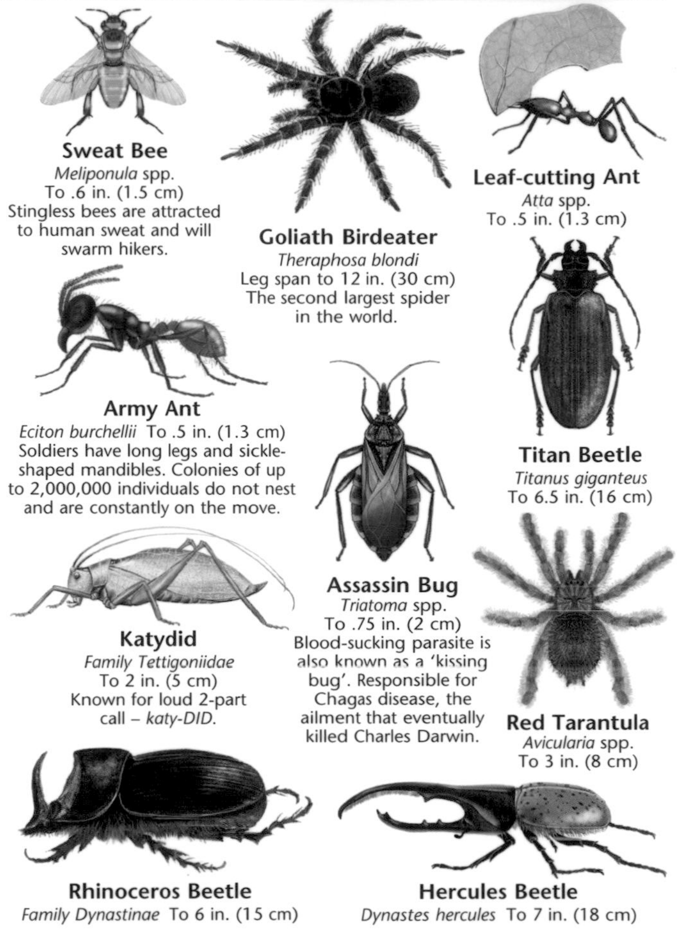

Sweat Bee
Meliponula spp.
To .6 in. (1.5 cm)
Stingless bees are attracted to human sweat and will swarm hikers.

Goliath Birdeater
Theraphosa blondi
Leg span to 12 in. (30 cm)
The second largest spider in the world.

Leaf-cutting Ant
Atta spp.
To .5 in. (1.3 cm)

Army Ant
Eciton burchellii To .5 in. (1.3 cm)
Soldiers have long legs and sickle-shaped mandibles. Colonies of up to 2,000,000 individuals do not nest and are constantly on the move.

Titan Beetle
Titanus giganteus
To 6.5 in. (16 cm)

Assassin Bug
Triatoma spp.
To .75 in. (2 cm)
Blood-sucking parasite is also known as a 'kissing bug'. Responsible for Chagas disease, the ailment that eventually killed Charles Darwin.

Katydid
Family Tettigoniidae
To 2 in. (5 cm)
Known for loud 2-part call – *katy-DID.*

Red Tarantula
Avicularia spp.
To 3 in. (8 cm)

Rhinoceros Beetle
Family Dynastinae To 6 in. (15 cm)

Hercules Beetle
Dynastes hercules To 7 in. (18 cm)

FISHES

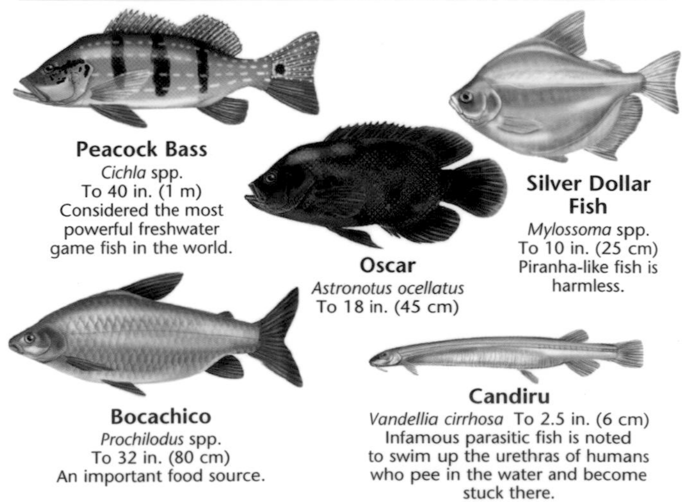

Peacock Bass
Cichla spp.
To 40 in. (1 m)
Considered the most powerful freshwater game fish in the world.

Silver Dollar Fish
Mylossoma spp.
To 10 in. (25 cm)
Piranha-like fish is harmless.

Oscar
Astronotus ocellatus
To 18 in. (45 cm)

Bocachico
Prochilodus spp.
To 32 in. (80 cm)
An important food source.

Candiru
Vandellia cirrhosa To 2.5 in. (6 cm)
Infamous parasitic fish is noted to swim up the urethras of humans who pee in the water and become stuck there.

FISHES

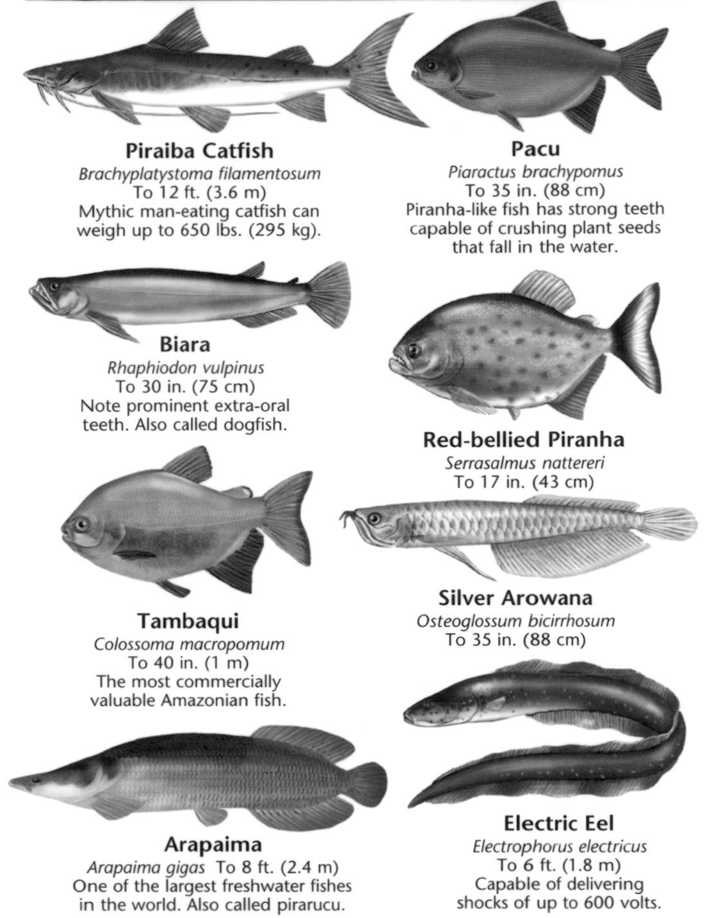

Piraiba Catfish
Brachyplatystoma filamentosum
To 12 ft. (3.6 m)
Mythic man-eating catfish can weigh up to 650 lbs. (295 kg).

Pacu
Piaractus brachypomus
To 35 in. (88 cm)
Piranha-like fish has strong teeth capable of crushing plant seeds that fall in the water.

Biara
Rhaphiodon vulpinus
To 30 in. (75 cm)
Note prominent extra-oral teeth. Also called dogfish.

Red-bellied Piranha
Serrasalmus nattereri
To 17 in. (43 cm)

Tambaqui
Colossoma macropomum
To 40 in. (1 m)
The most commercially valuable Amazonian fish.

Silver Arowana
Osteoglossum bicirrhosum
To 35 in. (88 cm)

Arapaima
Arapaima gigas To 8 ft. (2.4 m)
One of the largest freshwater fishes in the world. Also called pirarucu.

Electric Eel
Electrophorus electricus
To 6 ft. (1.8 m)
Capable of delivering shocks of up to 600 volts.

REPTILES & AMPHIBIANS

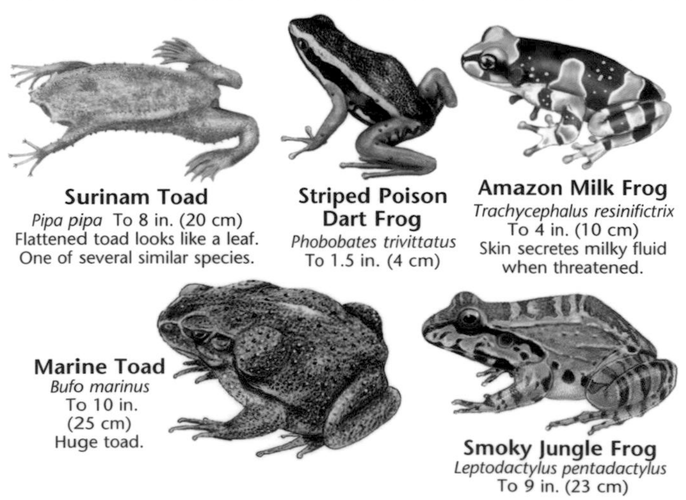

Surinam Toad
Pipa pipa To 8 in. (20 cm)
Flattened toad looks like a leaf. One of several similar species.

Striped Poison Dart Frog
Phobobates trivittatus
To 1.5 in. (4 cm)

Amazon Milk Frog
Trachycephalus resinifictrix
To 4 in. (10 cm)
Skin secretes milky fluid when threatened.

Marine Toad
Bufo marinus
To 10 in. (25 cm)
Huge toad.

Smoky Jungle Frog
Leptodactylus pentadactylus
To 9 in. (23 cm)

REPTILES & AMPHIBIANS

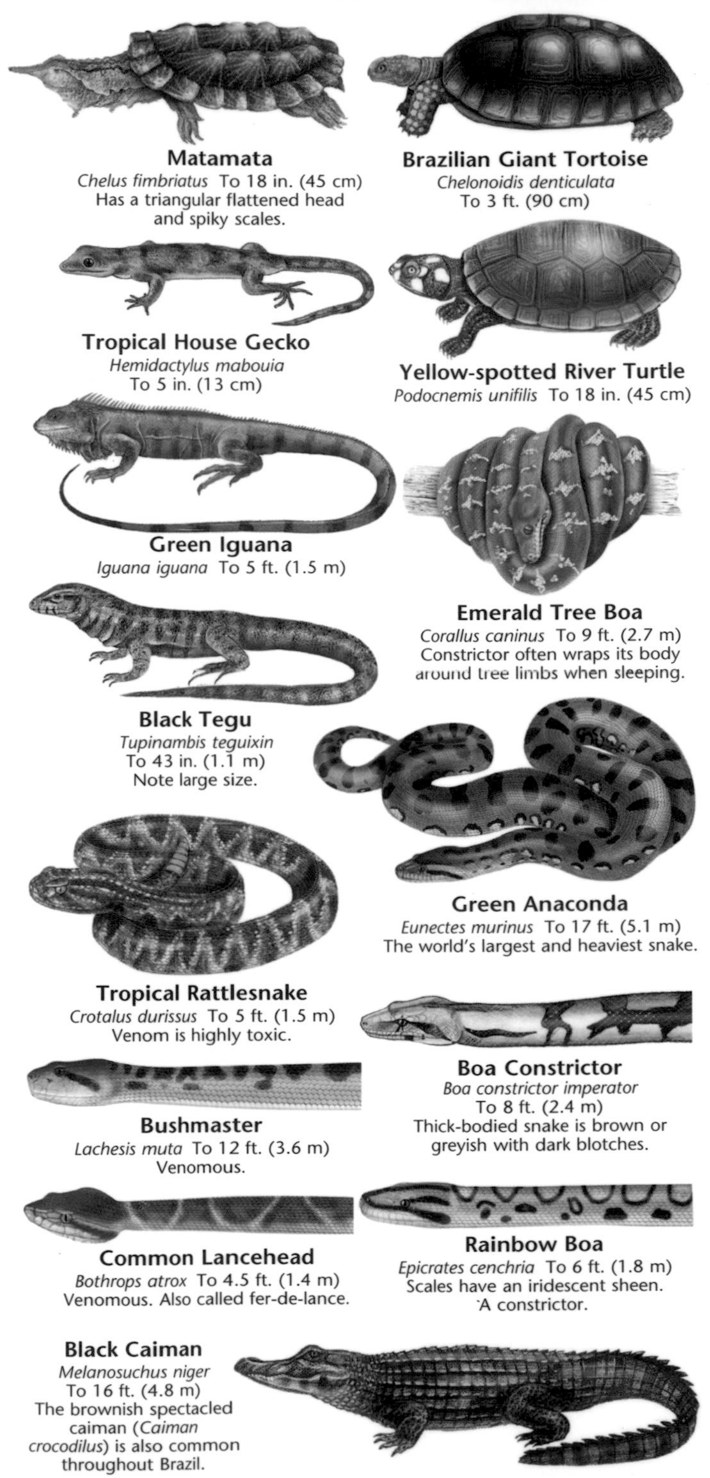

Matamata
Chelus fimbriatus To 18 in. (45 cm)
Has a triangular flattened head and spiky scales.

Brazilian Giant Tortoise
Chelonoidis denticulata
To 3 ft. (90 cm)

Tropical House Gecko
Hemidactylus mabouia
To 5 in. (13 cm)

Yellow-spotted River Turtle
Podocnemis unifilis To 18 in. (45 cm)

Green Iguana
Iguana iguana To 5 ft. (1.5 m)

Emerald Tree Boa
Corallus caninus To 9 ft. (2.7 m)
Constrictor often wraps its body around tree limbs when sleeping.

Black Tegu
Tupinambis teguixin
To 43 in. (1.1 m)
Note large size.

Green Anaconda
Eunectes murinus To 17 ft. (5.1 m)
The world's largest and heaviest snake.

Tropical Rattlesnake
Crotalus durissus To 5 ft. (1.5 m)
Venom is highly toxic.

Boa Constrictor
Boa constrictor imperator
To 8 ft. (2.4 m)
Thick-bodied snake is brown or greyish with dark blotches.

Bushmaster
Lachesis muta To 12 ft. (3.6 m)
Venomous.

Common Lancehead
Bothrops atrox To 4.5 ft. (1.4 m)
Venomous. Also called fer-de-lance.

Rainbow Boa
Epicrates cenchria To 6 ft. (1.8 m)
Scales have an iridescent sheen. A constrictor.

Black Caiman
Melanosuchus niger
To 16 ft. (4.8 m)
The brownish spectacled caiman (*Caiman crocodilus*) is also common throughout Brazil.

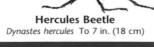

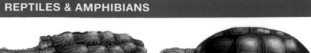

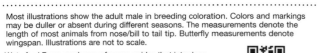

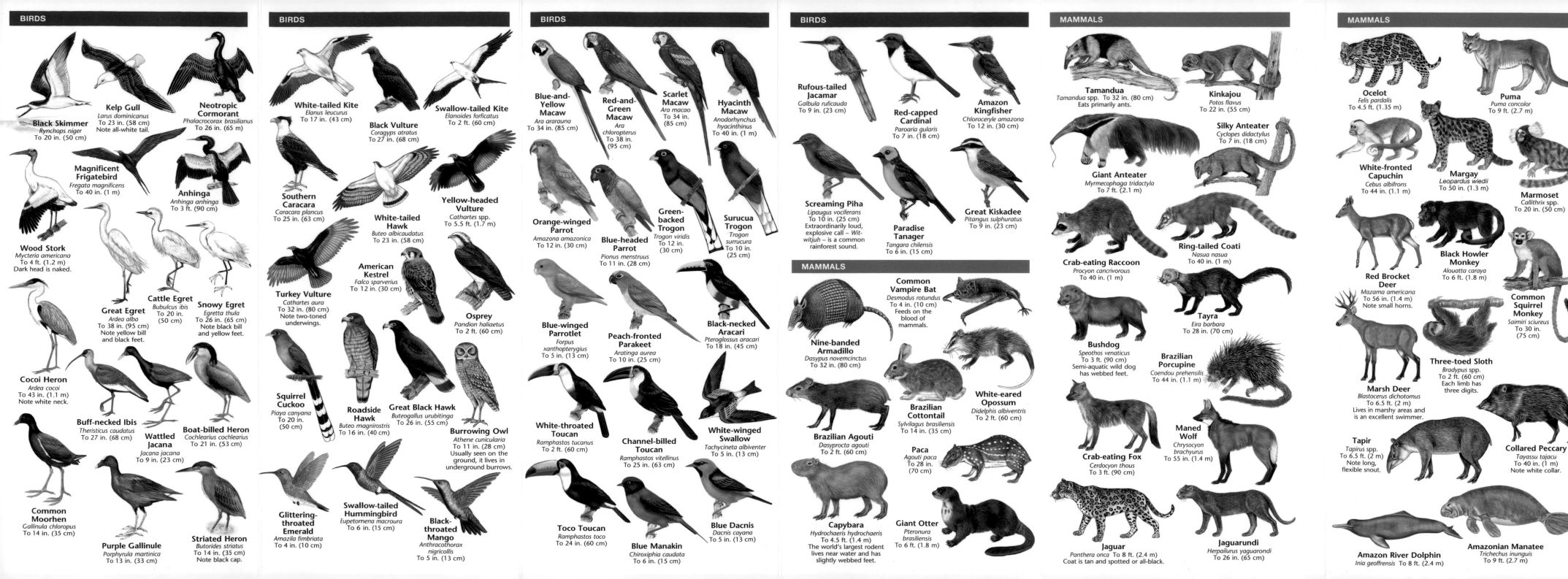

BIRDS

Black Skimmer
Rynchops niger
To 20 in. (50 cm)

Kelp Gull
Larus dominicanus
To 23 in. (58 cm)
Note all-white tail.

Neotropic Cormorant
Phalacrocorax brasilianus
To 26 in. (65 m)

Magnificent Frigatebird
Fregata magnificens
To 40 in. (1 m)

Anhinga
Anhinga anhinga
To 3 ft. (90 cm)

Wood Stork
Mycteria americana
To 4 ft. (1.2 m)
Dark head is naked.

Great Egret
Ardea alba
To 38 in. (95 cm)
Note yellow bill
and black feet.

Cattle Egret
Bubulcus ibis
To 20 in. (50 cm)

Snowy Egret
Egretta thula
To 26 in. (65 cm)
Note black bill
and yellow feet.

Cocoi Heron
Ardea cocoi
To 43 in. (1.1 m)
Note white neck.

Buff-necked Ibis
Theristicus caudatus
To 27 in. (68 cm)

Wattled Jacana
Jacana jacana
To 9 in. (23 cm)

Boat-billed Heron
Cochlearius cochlearius
To 21 in. (53 cm)

Common Moorhen
Gallinula chloropus
To 14 in. (35 cm)

Purple Gallinule
Porphyrula martinica
To 13 in. (33 cm)

Striated Heron
Butorides striatus
To 14 in. (35 cm)
Note black cap.

BIRDS

White-tailed Kite
Elanus leucurus
To 17 in. (43 cm)

Black Vulture
Coragyps atratus
To 27 in. (68 cm)

Swallow-tailed Kite
Elanoides forficatus
To 2 ft. (60 cm)

Southern Caracara
Caracara plancus
To 25 in. (63 cm)

White-tailed Hawk
Buteo albicaudatus
To 23 in. (58 cm)

Yellow-headed Vulture
Cathartes spp.
To 5.5 ft. (1.7 m)

Turkey Vulture
Cathartes aura
To 32 in. (80 cm)
Note two-toned
underwings.

American Kestrel
Falco sparverius
To 12 in. (30 cm)

Osprey
Pandion haliaetus
To 2 ft. (60 cm)

Squirrel Cuckoo
Piaya cayana
To 20 in. (50 cm)

Roadside Hawk
Buteo magnirostris
To 16 in. (40 cm)

Great Black Hawk
Buteogallus urubitinga
To 26 in. (55 cm)

Burrowing Owl
Athene cunicularia
To 11 in. (28 cm)
Usually seen on the
ground, it lives in
underground burrows.

Glittering-throated Emerald
Amazila fimbriata
To 4 in. (10 cm)

Swallow-tailed Hummingbird
Eupetomena macroura
To 6 in. (15 cm)

Black-throated Mango
Anthracothorax nigricollis
To 5 in. (13 cm)

BIRDS

Blue-and-Yellow Macaw
Ara ararauna
To 34 in. (85 cm)

Red-and-Green Macaw
Ara chloropterus
To 38 in. (95 cm)

Scarlet Macaw
Ara macao
To 34 in. (85 cm)

Hyacinth Macaw
Anodorhynchus hyacinthinus
To 40 in. (1 m)

Orange-winged Parrot
Amazona amazonica
To 12 in. (30 cm)

Blue-headed Parrot
Pionus menstruus
To 11 in. (28 cm)

Green-backed Trogon
Trogon viridis
To 12 in. (30 cm)

Surucua Trogon
Trogon surrucura
To 10 in. (25 cm)

Blue-winged Parrotlet
Forpus xanthopterygius
To 5 in. (13 cm)

Peach-fronted Parakeet
Aratinga aurea
To 10 in. (25 cm)

Black-necked Aracari
Pteroglossus aracari
To 18 in. (45 cm)

White-throated Toucan
Ramphastos tucanus
To 2 ft. (60 cm)

Channel-billed Toucan
Ramphastos vitellinus
To 25 in. (63 cm)

White-winged Swallow
Tachycineta albiventer
To 5 in. (13 cm)

Toco Toucan
Ramphastos toco
To 24 in. (60 cm)

Blue Manakin
Chiroxiphia caudata
To 6 in. (15 cm)

Blue Dacnis
Dacnis cayana
To 5 in. (13 cm)

BIRDS

Rufous-tailed Jacamar
Galbula ruficauda
To 9 in. (23 cm)

Red-capped Cardinal
Paroaria gularis
To 7 in. (18 cm)

Amazon Kingfisher
Chloroceryle amazona
To 12 in. (30 cm)

Screaming Piha
Lipaugus vociferans
To 10 in. (25 cm)
Extraordinarily loud,
explosive call – *Wit-
witjuh* – is a common
rainforest sound.

Paradise Tanager
Tangara chilensis
To 6 in. (15 cm)

Great Kiskadee
Pitangus sulphuratus
To 9 in. (23 cm)

MAMMALS

Common Vampire Bat
Desmodus rotundus
To 4 in. (10 cm)
Feeds on the
blood of
mammals.

Nine-banded Armadillo
Dasypus novemcinctus
To 32 in. (80 cm)

White-eared Opossum
Didelphis albiventris
To 2 ft. (60 cm)

Brazilian Cottontail
Sylvilagus brasiliensis
To 14 in. (35 cm)

Brazilian Agouti
Dasyprocta agouti
To 2 ft. (60 cm)

Paca
Agouti paca
To 28 in. (70 cm)

Capybara
Hydrochaeris hydrochaeris
To 4.5 ft. (1.4 m)
The world's largest rodent
lives near water and has
slightly webbed feet.

Giant Otter
Pteronura brasiliensis
To 6 ft. (1.8 m)

MAMMALS

Tamandua
Tamandua spp. To 32 in. (80 cm)
Eats primarily ants.

Kinkajou
Potos flavus
To 22 in. (55 cm)

Giant Anteater
Myrmecophaga tridactyla
To 7 ft. (2.1 m)

Silky Anteater
Cyclopes didactylus
To 7 in. (18 cm)

Crab-eating Raccoon
Procyon cancrivorous
To 40 in. (1 m)

Ring-tailed Coati
Nasua nasua
To 40 in. (1 m)

Bushdog
Speothos venaticus
To 3 ft. (90 cm)
Semi-aquatic wild dog
has webbed feet.

Tayra
Eira barbara
To 28 in. (70 cm)

Brazilian Porcupine
Coendou prehensilis
To 44 in. (1.1 m)

Crab-eating Fox
Cerdocyon thous
To 3 ft. (90 cm)

Maned Wolf
Chrysocyon brachyurus
To 55 in. (1.4 m)

Jaguar
Panthera onca To 8 ft. (2.4 m)
Coat is tan and spotted or all-black.

Jaguarundi
Herpailurus yaguarondi
To 26 in. (65 cm)

MAMMALS

Ocelot
Felis pardalis
To 4.5 ft. (1.35 m)

Puma
Puma concolor
To 9 ft. (2.7 m)

White-fronted Capuchin
Cebus albifrons
To 44 in. (1.1 m)

Margay
Leopardus wiedii
To 50 in. (1.3 m)

Marmoset
Callithrix spp.
To 20 in. (50 cm)

Red Brocket Deer
Mazama americana
To 56 in. (1.4 m)
Note small horns.

Black Howler Monkey
Alouatta caraya
To 6 ft. (1.8 m)

Common Squirrel Monkey
Saimiri sciureus
To 30 in. (75 cm)

Three-toed Sloth
Bradypus spp.
To 2 ft. (60 cm)
Each limb has
three digits.

Marsh Deer
Blastocerus dichotomus
To 6.5 ft. (2 m)
Lives in marshy areas and
is an excellent swimmer.

Tapir
Tapirus spp.
To 6.5 ft. (2 m)
Note long,
flexible snout.

Collared Peccary
Tayassu tajacu
To 40 in. (1 m)
Note white collar.

Amazon River Dolphin
Inia geoffrensis
To 8 ft. (2.4 m)

Amazonian Manatee
Trichechus inunguis
To 9 ft. (2.7 m)